The Vatican-Jesuit-Global Conspiracy

by Dr. Ronald Cooke

ISBN: 978-2-925369-90-5
Printed in the USA.

PREFACE

This is the fourth in a series of booklets on the Vatican in the Western world today. In this booklet we try to sketch the role that the Vatican plays in world politics today and the goal and plan it has for the world. We also look at the enormous financial resources that the Vatican possesses and the billions more which are at its disposal.

We also look at the part that the Jesuits play in helping to implement the goal of the Vatican. In our travels and teaching we find that there is almost a total blackout concerning the sinister aspirations of the Vatican and the Jesuits. Men who purport to write on the great conspiracy that is out to control the world not only never mention the Vatican, but if they do, they make the Vatican out to be the target of the conspiracy rather than the originator of the conspiracy.

It is obvious to anyone who is even remotely interested in the Vatican conspiracy that times have certainly changed the attitudes of Protestant Christians toward the Jesuits. The word "Jesuit" used to conjure up in the minds of those who heard it a malevolent and satanic rictus. But times have changed. Today Jesuits are accorded reverence and respect in all segments of western society, and yes, even allowed back into Eastern society after being banned from countries like China for almost thirty years.

Former President Nixon used a Jesuit to write his speeches. Jesuits are leading lights in the modern irenic dialogue of the ecumenical movement so that at least in the United States an aura of respectability now surrounds the workings of the Jesuits. Not all Americans or even all American Roman Catholics are impressed with the Jesuits, but the plans of the Vatican Hierarchy are proceeding along clearly defined lines no matter whether some Roman Catholics may approve or not. The Vatican and the Jesuits have the same goal in mind. They are both working to bring the world to the feet of the Roman Pontiff. The Jesuits have been backing the Marxists in some trouble spots of the world, especially in Latin America. The Pope wants to retain the close backing he enjoys from men like Ronald Reagan; therefore, he pretended to reprimand the Jesuits for working with the Marxists in Central America. As we will see later, the Marxists in Central America, as in Northern Ireland, all have good Roman Catholic credentials.

What most people do not realize is that the Jesuits are the C.I.A. of the Vatican. That is, just as Washington often seems to conflict with, and disavow some of the covert activities of the C.I.A especially when they are going to prove embarrassing, so the Vatican from time to time will appear to disavow the activities of the Jesuits. In actuality just as Washington many times secretly hopes for the success of some clandestine operation of the C.I.A. although publicly disavowing any knowledge of it, so the Vatican hopes for the success of the Jesuits while publicly reprimanding them to appease those who are disturbed by their intrigue.

So although there may appear to be friction between the Jesuits and the Vatican, the friction has nothing whatsoever to do with Marxism per se as the American news media constantly affirms, it has to do with the possible break of some of the Marx·ists with the Vatican power structure, which might occur in coun·tries like Nicaragua. The Vatican lost Cuba because it misjudged Fidel Castro, who at one time was a faithful son of the Church. It does not want to make the same mistake again with Ernesto Cardenal and his Roman Catholic henchmen in Nicaragua. So the preemptive moves of the Pope in Central America today are primarily self-serving. The Pope realizes that much government-al control will be lost in Central America if the "church" does not go along with the Marxist liberation movements fomented by "church" leaders. On the other hand if the Pope appears to sup-port the Marxist liberation movements openly, he will lose the sup-port of the United States in Latin America. So the present Pope gives the impression that he is against Marxism by calling upon the Jesuits to get out of politics in Latin America and by summon-ing the Brazilian liberation theologian Leonardo Boff to Rome for an investigation.

These moves and others, which the present Pope is making, get mixed reviews in the U. S. press, but as Yallup points out in his recent book, *IN GOD'S NAME,* this Pope came to the Vatican with the attitude "business as usual," meaning that all the cor-ruption which the former Pope, who was murdered, wanted cleaned up, would continue.

The present Pope is a master politician, so he has spoken out against Marxism to retain the support of the United States in Poland. It is plainly a part of his overall strategy, a strategy which has always played both ends against the middle. The Pope backs the Marxist-oriented liberation movements of Latin America to the hilt as long as they remain subservient to the overall goals of the Vatican. It was to reinforce this subservience that he met with the Jesuits.

The Vatican realizes that it has lost out completely in most of Latin America if it does not back the Marxist revolutionaries, 99% of whom are Roman Catholics. So when the Pope visited the area, he alluded to the struggles for justice and human rights, which were going on in that part of the world. However, since the United States looks with concern on the Marxist revolutionaries, the Pope has since shifted course again and pretended to reprimand the clergy, who were, and are, involved in this region.

The C.I.A. of the papacy are without a doubt the Jesuits. They are working night and day to further the global aspirations of the Vatican. Their zeal and persistence are as great as they ever were even though they enjoy much more respectability than they once did. We try to show with documented evidence that the Vatican-Jesuit intrigue, far from being a "protestant myth," is a contemporary phenomenon, which is still functioning in the latter half of the twentieth-century.

Ronald Cooke
Manahath School of Theology
Hollidaysburg, Pennsylvania
1985

CONTENTS

THE JESUITS IN HISTORY

The true church of the Lord Jesus Christ has suffered reproach and endured persecution in almost every age since Stephen was martyred. In the early years of the church to confess Christ invited persecution and martyrdom. As the years rolled by and the church gained more power, it was not long until the church was doing the persecuting instead of being persecuted.

Augustine was one of the first, but certainly not the last, to advocate the necessity of force to extirpate error. As Farrar points out: "His writings became the Bible of the inquisition."[1] So from then on, inquisitorial methods became part and parcel of Rome's intrigues although stridently denied by some contemporary writers.

Martin Luther was used of God to set forth the liberating doctrine of justification by faith in the finished work of Christ and so dealt a death blow to Roman Catholicism. For this great Biblical doctrine destroys completely the whole-sacramentarian-good-works-priestly enterprise known as Roman Catholicism. Since the time of Luther the Roman institution has been working day and night to overthrow Bible Protestantism and return the "separated brethren" to the one true fold—the Vatican. No greater effort has been made than that made by the Jesuits. The Society of Jesus, founded by Loyola, has been at the origin of many conspiracies directed against Protestantism. They are documented conspiracies, not figments of an over active imagination. So it is nothing short of amazing when Gary Allen, who claims to be an authority in the field of conspiracy, calls in Pedro Arrupe to substantiate his thesis that a conspiracy exists. At the time that Allen wrote ten years ago, Pedro Arrupe was the head of the Jesuits.

The Jesuits are famous in history for their conspiracies, intrigues, assassinations, and their undying hatred of the Protestant Reformation. Pedro Arrupe was the head of an organization which every well informed Protestant knows was the main force behind the Counter Reformation. The Counter-Reformation sought by every means, fair or foul, to overthrow and undo the work of the glorious Protestant Reformation.

If there were no other reason to be against the Jesuits but this, that they attempted wherever possible to stop or hinder the true work of revival and gospel enlightenment in the church, it would be more than enough. But there are many more reasons than this. So for anyone claiming to be knowledgeable in the field of conspiracy to align himself with the head of the Jesuits is a severe blow, to say the least, to his credibility. Yet thousands of fundamental and conservative preachers speak constantly about Allen's "Insider" conspiracy without once stopping to consider the work of the Jesuits and their sponsor, the Vatican.

The Jesuits were so evil that they were feared even by Roman Catholic kings! MacPherson notes:

> The (Roman) Catholic king of Portugal says: it cannot be but that the licentiousness introduced by the Jesuits, of which the three leading features are falsehood, murder and perjury, deprive the laws of their power, destroy the submission of subjects, allow individuals the liberty of killing, calumniating, lying, and forswearing themselves as their advantage may dictate.[2]

McKinley adds his testimony to that of MacPherson.

> This society which has dared to appropriate to itself the Name, which is above every name, by calling itself, "The Order of Jesus," deserved rather from the nature of its doctrines and from the work it has done in the world to be called the Order of Satan.[3]

Even the secular historian, W. E. Lunt, whose text was used for years in American colleges and universities, recognized the conspiracies of the Jesuits.

> In this development the English Catholics had no small part...They were not a serious political menace until 1580 when two Jesuits came to England and began to plot with the Spanish ambassador...to place Mary on the throne. From that time Catholic plots were continually being hatched. Some had as their method a rebellion aided by foreign invasion while others sought their object by the simple mode of Elizabeth's assassination. None of the plots succeeded... Walsingham...laid bare the plots....and arrested several of the conspirators.[4]

The Jesuits actually became so powerful and overbearing that they were disbanded by none other than the pope himself. In 1773 Ganganelli, who succeeded Clement XIII, issued a papal bull in which he declared them suppressed and extinct and their statutes annulled. They remained suppressed for forty years, but in 1814 Pius VII issued a bull solemnly restablishing the society under the constitutions of "St. Ignatius."

The fact that the society was held in such disrepute even by its own institution is certainly not much of a recommendation for its evil practices. Yet, the man who headed this society when Gary Allen wrote his book, *"NONE DARE CALL IT CONSPIRACY,"* was called in by Allen to corroborate the fact that an international conspiracy exists. It is obvious that it is very easy to postulate a Bilderberger, Insider, or Trilateralist type of conspiracy without generating any animosity among the general public. Everyone and anyone can identify against a few rich evil men lurking in the shadows and working to take over the world. But to identify religious men as conspirators causes millions of people to bridle in anger and disbelief.

It is obvious that very few people know anything about the Jesuits today. Let us look at the organization that Ignatius of Loyola brought into being. There were several steps through which every well-trained Jesuit was to pass before he was graduated from his training.

1. The Spiritual Exercises.

These were undertaken with the object of inducing among other things a state of complete subjection of the will.[5]

2. If the trainee passed the first test, he was invited to become a novice.

From this time on, he is excluded from all earthly friends and is to have no will of his own as to his future. He is to put himself in the hands of his director as the interpreter of heaven toward him. Complete obedience is the thing that is absolutely required. His conscience must never assert itself in opposition to his superiors. Newman notes: "Absolute destruction of individual will and conscience is aimed at and to a great extent accomplished."[6]

Can anyone imagine a better base upon which to build a global conspiracy than complete and unquestioning obedience? In every small conspiracy about which details can be studied, one of the primary goals is to get each conspirator to give his unquestioning and complete obedience to the plan.

The Novitiate usually lasts two years. If the novice is found to possess the right qualities, he is accepted as a Scholar. Notice the weeding out process that continues all through the entire program. Only the most dedicated make it through to the final stages of the Society.

The Scholar now undergoes a protracted course of training in various branches of knowledge. Attention is paid to the cultivation of a sound physical make-up. If the Scholar is able to meet the requirements of this stage, he becomes a Coadjutor. Those who attain this rank are to devote themselves wholeheartedly to the advancement of the society. They serve as priests, missionaries, teachers and businessmen for the society.

The next rung on the ecclesiastical ladder is a group called the Professed. These are composed of a small proportion of the Coadjutors who have proved themselves and have been tested as to their complete trustworthiness regarding the aims of the society. It is from this group the officers of the society are drawn. They are the ones who are entrusted with its secrets. Watchcare is another important part of the society. Each member including the general is responsible to another, and according to Newman:

> to whom he must regularly make confession of his inmost thoughts, and who is required to exercize a watchcare over him and to report every deviation from rectitude, according to the standards of the body.[7]

The aim of the Order was, according to Ignatius, the promotion of the greater glory of God. According to Newman:

> The greater glory of God was identified by them in the most absolute way with the world wide and undisputed dominion of the Roman Catholic Church.[8]

The methods of the Order are well known. In most cases the Jesuits deny the charges against them. But it has been charged that they infiltrate into places of power using as their watchword, the phrase "the end justifies the means." The fact that they deny such actions should not cause any surprise since that is part and parcel of their method of operation.

Their ethical system allows all kinds of loopholes by which to escape any situation that might cause embarrassment to the Society or to the Roman Catholic Church. The society did openly defend their recommendation that tyrants should be assassinated.[9] Their doctrine of Probabilism, although rejected by some members, nevertheless secured papal recognition. Their ability to escape responsibility by the method of "directing the intention" also demonstrates that the phrase "the end justifies the means," although never appearing in their writings, is there in their purpose as plain as day.

Another equally objectionable doctrine was their teaching on mental reservation or restriction, whereby one, without burden to his conscience, might tell a downright lie provided the word or clause that would make it true is in his mind.

> Thus, one accused of having committed a certain act last week in a certain place may swear that he was not there, reserving the statement "this morning."[10]

The Secret Instructions, supposed to be the frank directions of the generals to the provincials and others involving unscrupulous commands, can no longer be used. The genuineness of the document has been denied by the society. It was first published in 1612, and, if not genuine, was probably the production of the ex-Jesuit Hieronymus Zaorowski.[11] However, as Newman cogently reasons:

> The repudiation of the work by the Society is, of course, no conclusive evidence of its spuriousness. It has been the consistent policy of the society from the beginning to deny everything disadvantageous to the church or to itself.[12]

The supreme end as noted above was the greater glory of God. So any superior can declare an end, however diabolical, to involve the greater glory of God, and command his inferior to use any means whatever for the accomplishment of this end, including, as Newman points out: "deceit, theft, and even murder; and the inferior must unquestioningly obey."[13]

Hodge also points out in his work the notoriety which the Jesuits attained through their principle of mental reservation.

> The doctrine that the character of an act depended solely

on the intention. If the intention be good, the act is good; whether it be falsehood, perjury, murder, or any other conceivable crime. Pascal quotes the Jesuit moralist Escobar as laying down the general principle, "that promises are not binding unless there was an intention of keeping them, at the time they were made." On the same principle, that the intention determines the character of the act, the murder of Henry III, in 1589; of the Prince of Orange in 1584; of Henry IV, of France in 1610; and especially the massacres on the feast of St. Bartholomew, were all justified,.[14]

Gordon Liddy, who was also educated by the Jesuits, used the same type of reasoning for justifying his part in the Nixon Watergate scandal. It is very significant that Liddy, who now claims he does not believe in God, nevertheless uses the various definitions of the Roman moralists to justify murder.

It is the same rationale by which I was willing to obey an order to kill Jack Anderson. But I would do so only after satisfying myself that it was: (a) an order from legitimate authority; (b) a question of malum prohibitum; and (c) a rational response to the problem. [15]

Once we allow the reasoning of the Jesuits to prevail, then murder becomes a viable means of policy if we feel that it is necessary. It is tragic that many fundamental and evangelical Christians agree with this type of reasoning today, showing that Jesuitical casuistry has made vast strides since the sixteenth century.

We believe in capital punishment. We do not believe, however, that any man has the right to be judge, jury and executioner. Once allow this type of thinking, and Tomas Torquemada and the Inquisition will not be far away.

The Jesuits were well received in Italy and in Portugal at first. However in Spain, Charles V was opposed to their methods and to their ideas of papal absolutism. Leading Roman Catholic Spanish theologians such as Melchior Canus denounced them as the forerunners of anti-Christ foretold by the Apostle in II Timothy 3:2.

In France they met with opposition but finally gained a foothold and permission to establish a college at Clermont. In Lyons, their presence and preaching resulted in the burning of the books and churches of the Huguenots. It is probable that the Massacre of St. Bartholomew's Day was due in some measure to their influence.[16]

In England, Trevelyan says of the Jesuits that their policy aimed "at the overthrow of the existing regime and the forcible extirpation of Protestantism."[17] A likelier group to originate a global conspiracy would indeed be difficult to find. Their zeal knew no bounds. They were and are the heart and soul of the Counter-Reformation. As Newman, the great Southern Baptist Historian, points out:

> The chief means that were used by the Counter-Reformation from this time onward (1541) were the Council of Trent, The Society of Jesus, and the Inquisition...These means of fortifying the church and repressing heresy are closely interlinked. The Council of Trent, especially in its later and more important phases, and the establishment and working of the Inquisition, like the policy of the papacy in general, were due to Jesuit influence.[18]

So for someone to call in Pedro Arrupe to comment on the possible existence of a conspiracy is like calling in Adolf Hitler to comment on the possible existence of Nazism. It is better to go with known facts about conspiracy than to hint at hidden conspiracies which may not even exist.

The Jesuits were indefatigable in their efforts to restore Romanism to its former glory in the areas where Protestantism had gained a foothold. Von Ranke tells of the return of the idolatry of Romanism to parts of Germany.

> In Cologne it was again an honor to wear the Rosary. Relics were once more held up to public reverence in Treves, where for many years no one had ventured to exhibit them... the youth of Ingolstadt belonging to the Jesuit school walked... on a pilgrimage...in order to be strengthened for their confirmation "by the dew that dropped from the tomb of St. Walpurgis."[19]

The Jesuits were the first effective counter action against the progress of Protestantism that the Roman Catholic Church was able to wage. Yet few Protestants then, and now, fail to realize the eternal issues which are at stake in this battle. Grace and idolatrous works are mutually exclusive. Error is only defeated by the proclamation of the truth. It is never defeated by compromise, half-truths, or a failure to recognize its existence.

REFERENCES

1. Farrar, F. W. *History of Interpretation,* Baker Book House, Reprint, p. 235
2. MacPherson, Hector, *The Jesuits in History,* Edinburgh, Scotland. 1914, pp. 104-105
3. Ash, McKinley, *The Antichrist,* Blackwood, N.J. p. 91
4. Lunt, W.E., *History of England,* p. 378
5. Newman, Albert Henry, *A Manual of Church History, Vol. II,* Philadelphia, 1947, p. 369
6. Ibid., p. 370
7. Ibid., p. 371
8. Ibid., p. 372
9. loc cit.
10. Ibid., p. 372
11. loc. cit
12. Ibid., p. 378
13. Ibid., p. 379
14. Hodge, Charles, *Systematic Theology, Vol. III,* N.Y. 1873, pp. 445-446
15. Liddy, G. Gordon, *Will,* Dell Pub. Co. 1981, p. 291
16. Newman, p. 381
17. Trevelyan, G.M., *History of England, Vol II.,* Doubleday, N.Y. 1953, p. 158
18. Newman, p. 355
19. Von Ranke, Leopold, *History of the Popes, Vol II,* Collier, N.Y. 1901, p. 23

THE JESUITS TODAY

Many Americans, of course, while paying half-hearted attention to such historical matters are convinced that although there may be some misdeeds in history, the Jesuits of the present have changed. Others seem to believe that the intrigue of the Jesuits is needed today to counteract the communist menace.

G. Gordon Liddy of Watergate fame was taught by the Jesuits, and nowhere does he apologize for their teachings or for his philosophy of life which is based on the Jesuit teaching that the end justifies the means. In fact, he unashamedly advocates this teaching as the only way that America can survive.

In his autobiography he states:

> Fordham was a feast for the mind and a challenge to the spirit. To begin with, it was still under the absolute control of the Jesuits...As much as I had admired the German Benedictines, I admired the Jesuits more...
>
> The Society of Jesus was something special—the shock troop of the Catholic Church.[1]

He goes on to say that Heinrich Himmler used it as the model for his dreaded black-uniformed SS in Hitler's Germany and that the SS swore a special oath of loyalty to the Fuhrer, just as the highest order of the Jesuits swore a special oath of loyalty to the Pope. Liddy says later on that "just as I do, John Sirica believes the end justifies the means."[2]

The Jesuits obviously have gained respectability in our time. They have come a long way since John Adams, the second President of the United States, wrote in a letter to Thomas Jefferson: "If ever there was a body of men who merited eternal damnation on earth and in Hell, it is this Society of Loyola."[3]

John G. Schmitz, who ran for President on the American Party ticket a few years ago, was educated by the Jesuits. His education by the Jesuits was put forward as something in his favor rather than a liability. He also wrote the foreword to Gary Allen's book, "NONE DARE CALL IT CONSPIRACY." So we live in remarkable times when Jesuit trained leaders can write about conspiracy and be accepted not only by the general public, but by professed conservative Protestant Christianity.

Jerry Brown, the Governor of California, who has twice sought the presidential nomination, was also educated by the Jesuits. Again, this was not something considered a liability, rather it was advertised as proof of his moral fiber and strength of character. Times certainly have changed in America.

Harry Reasoner, as he was signing off his nationally televised newscast a few years ago, also demonstrated how far the Jesuits have come in gaining complete acceptance in the United States. He told a joke about three orders in the Roman Catholic Church. It went something like this. The Dominicans, the Franciscans and the Jesuits were all arguing about which order God loved the most. They went down to the altar and were told that they would receive the answer the next day. When they went back the next day, there was a note on the altar which said, "I love you all equally." Signed, God, S.J. Harry signed off chuckling to himself. While we can appreciate a joke, we do not consider the Jesuits a laughing matter. For if the Bible is true, and we believe it is, then the Jesuit idea of salvation by works, masses, and ceremonies has led millions, and is still leading millions, to a lost eternity.

To those who cherish biblical truth and the freedom to preach the true Gospel, the rise of the Jesuits to a place of complete acceptance and indeed power in the United States today does not bode well for the future of this great land. Everything that Protestant Americans hold dear will be forfeited if these men ever gain the ascendancy in this land.

The greatest proof of all that the Jesuits have indeed gained complete respectability in the United States today is the startling fact that a man claiming to outline the global shadowy conspiracy that threatens the world should call in the leader of the Jesuits to substantiate and corroborate his thesis. No one informed in the area of church history would ever do such a thing unless he believed that the time had come when the Jesuits were no longer suspect themselves. Apparently, Gary Allen believes that this time has arrived. Millions of conservatively oriented Americans who agree with Allen are either totally ignorant of the historical record or believe that the Jesuits have changed. It can be said without fear of contradiction that whether or not one agrees with the idea of a Jesuit Conspiracy, no Protestant who has studied church history would ever call in the leader of the Jesuits to corroborate his view of conspiracy.

The Jesuits have not only gained complete respectability in the United States today, but they have also gained great power. They own a controlling interest in the Bank of America as well as other financial interests. They are thus able to influence Roman Catholic politicians to serve the ends of the Roman Catholic Church more vigorously. (We will look at the Vatican's vast financial empire in more detail in the next chapter.)

The Jesuits were involved in intrigue at the highest levels of the United States government. During the administration of John F. Kennedy, the Jesuits had access to the most powerful office in the world. The Rev. James Vizzard, an American Jesuit who served as a labor lobbyist in Washington, disclosed that in 1963 he was having lunch with another Jesuit, Roger Vekemans, a Belgian priest on assignment to Chile, when a White House car picked Vekemans up and took him to a meeting with President Kennedy, Attorney General Robert Kennedy, and C.I.A. Director John Mc-Cone, certainly three of the most powerful men in the world at that time.

> Vizzard said: "Roger came back with a big smile on his face and said, 'I got $10 million—$5 million overt from AID (Agency for International Development) and $5 million covert from the C.I.A.' "[4]

Since that time some other investigations have shown that there was a Roman Catholic bishop on the payroll of the C.I.A. in Vietnam as late as 1971, that millions of dollars were sent by the U.S. government to help the Jesuits in Chile, a country then beset by assassinations and intrigue and still embroiled in murder and mayhem, and at this writing still controlled by a Roman Catholic military dictatorship.

Only the tip of the iceberg has ever been seen. It is obvious that the subject of Jesuit intrigue in the C.I.A. has so far never been explored in any depth whatsoever. Licio Gelli whom some writers believe is the man who helps hold together the Vatican conspiracy, which is out to control the world, has strong links with the C.I.A. He is called Il Burattinaco—The Puppetmaster. Yallop says of him, "Gelli was the puppetmaster with a few thousand strings. The strings appear to have led everywhere, to the heart of the Vatican, to the White House, to presidential palaces in a wide range of countries."[5]

Gelli was the man who bought Exocet Missiles from France for Argentina in its war with Britain. Yallop says that the Vatican indirectly funded Celli through Calvi and the Bianco Ambrosiano. Gelli was an honored guest at Reagan's presidential inauguration. Gelli, of course, has strong ties with Michele Sindona. He is the head of P2, the mysterious organization founded in Italy which functions in Argentina, Venezuela, Paraguay, France, Portugal, Nicaragua, Switzerland, and the United States. It interlocks with the Mafia in Italy, Cuba and the United States and also with military regimes in South America, and also with the C.I.A. and reaches right into the heart of the Vatican.[6]

So the tentacles of the Vatican power structure spread worldwide. Men come and go, but the organizations of the papacy perpetuate themselves and have done so for more than a thousand years, making the Vatican the source of the most formidable intrigue in world history. When Yallop sought to find out about the mysterious death of Pope John Paul, he said that:

> The fact that men and women living within the heart of the Roman Catholic Church (Vatican City) cannot speak openly and be identified, is an eloquent comment on the state of affairs within the Vatican.[7]

The Pope has called for the Jesuits to cease from their intrigue in Central America. On March 2, 1982, over one hundred Jesuit Provincial Superiors, the leaders of the Order, were called to Rome for discussions with "Father" Paolo Dezza, the man the Pope had appointed to oversee the Order in 1981.

The Jesuits were accused by the Pope himself of engaging in "political activism under the guise of religious duties."[8] In the same article the Jesuits were reported to be "one of the primary groups controlling both extremes in Central America."[9]

So the Jesuits are still in the thick of the murders and assassinations which are being carried out by both sides in the war in E Salvador. The Pope, like others before him, is trying to curb their zeal to keep all factions in the war subservient to Rome.

With the rise of the death squads like those in Ulster, the focus of world opinion is forcing the Pope to do something to at least give the impression that he is not in favor of the murders and killings in El Salvador. But the high degree of Jesuit involvement with the extremists on both sides of the conflict in El Salvador is now a matter of public record.

The Extremists on both sides of this conflict are Roman Catholics. Roman Catholic Marxists are fighting Roman Catholic conservatives. The church is charting a course that will enable it to identify with whoever wins in the end. The Acting Archbishop said recently, "The left has lost its struggle against the government and therefore the influential church here must stay in a neutral, centrist position."[10] The acting Archbishop made this statement after the killing of 3 Marxist nuns, 10 Marxist priests, and the assassination of Marxist Archbishop Oscar A. Romero. It was after this reign of terror by the Roman Catholic conservatives that the "influential church withdrew to its neutral, centrist position." It is obvious that the conservative wing of Romanism, which has a large representation among the North American clergy, is backing the right-wing fighters in El Salvador. However, some local Roman Catholic leaders are calling for the United States to back off in El Salvador. So it looks like another capitulation to Marxism is shaping up in Central America.

Latin America sits on a veritable power keg because Romanism, which has been entrenched there for four hundred years, has not brought a scintilla of freedom or justice to the oppressed millions who live below the border of the United States and well below the abject poverty line. Romanism has managed to keep the multiplied millions in such a state of miserable existence that we have no hesitation in saying that if Americans rebelled against George III for his repression, they would have rebelled long ago against almost every government in Latin America.

Instead the United States bolsters the repression of Rome all over Latin America, paving the way for the inevitable revolution and "liberation" promised by the Marxists. It is time the United States stopped identifying with Romanism. But while the massive propaganda machine of Rome churns out its slanted coverage of the news, public opinion in the United States will enable Rome to keep its stranglehold on the people either by repressive fascist governments as in Chile or repressive Marxists government dictatorships as in Nicaragua. Not only that, but the Vatican wants the U.S. to fund the "rebuilding" of this region while the "church" retains control over the people.

Ed Asner has been blasted by many in the U.S. for his stand

against U.S. involvement in El Salvador. Asner, of course, was the popular Hollywood actor in several recent television series. He was hounded into silence by being labelled a Communist or leftist or worse if that were possible. What was it that brought down the wrath of a large section of the American public upon Ed Asner? Simply because he spoke out on the situation in El Salvador. What is the situation in El Salvador that Asner deplores? It is the conservative Roman Catholic death squads massacring hundreds of civilians under the guise of eliminating leftists. It is amazing the leftists that are in the world today. Everyone who opposes Romanism is a leftist, Marxist or Communist. The possibility of a Protestant Christian opposing Rome is so remote today that apparently it is safe to label everyone who opposes Romanism as a leftist. (A few years ago one conservative west coast commentator even called Paisley a communist.)

This is the propaganda that Asner was challenging, that anyone who opposes the totalitarian poverty and ignorance-producing regimes of Latin America today must be a leftist. There are leftists to be sure who challenge Rome's 400 year reign of terror and extreme poverty, and the sad thing that should be noted but never is, is that there are few Americans who would not have challenged such regimes long, long ago!! The poor peons ground into the dirt for centuries look to the U.S. to liberate them, and all they get in return is the backing of the rotten tyrannical dictatorships by the powerful U.S. government, a mere lackey of the Roman Catholic lobby in Washington. So they turn to whoever will help them in their struggle for some semblance of freedom. It is one of the great tragedies of our times that the only choice left to the people of Latin America in many cases is between Romanism on one side and Marxism on the other, and the Marxism even is the Jesuit brand. They are never given the choice of choosing neither Romanism nor Marxism but Protestantism. Protestantism has become so weak and has been betrayed by so many lily-livered compromisers that there is no viable choice left to many of the peoples of the world. Yet when the world is examined, Protestant countries with but few exceptions are the only ones where even a semblance of freedom remains.

Sister Ann Gormly, associate director of the U.S. Catholic Mission Association, in commenting on some of the allegations made against the Sandinista government in Nicaragua said, "I hear of no limitations to the work of the church in Nicaragua." She also said that it is good to have four churchmen in high government posts in Nicaragua.[11] So although there are many uncertain sounds emanating from Nicaragua, the Vatican is deeply embroiled in the present government, and no amount of double-talk can dispel the fact that at least four sons of the "church" have the highest posts in the Sandinista government.

We certainly do not try to play down the fact that there are apparently deep rifts between some local priests and nuns who side with the poor and believe in "liberation theology" and the present Pope, who is opposed to them. But the bottom line is loyalty. If the leftist leaning clergy and political leaders promise to remain loyal to the Vatican in all their intrigues, then the Pope will overlook their Marxist ideology even as a former Pope overlooked the Nazi ideology of Hitler and his henchmen.

One modern writer commenting on the situation in Nicaragua said:

> The major target of the U.S. is the Sandinista government of Nicaragua, which is now considered a Marxist regime. The truth of the matter is that there are more Jesuits and Jesuit-controlled individuals in the Sandinista government than there are individuals in the whole of Nicaragua who have gone beyond the first chapter of Marx's Capital.[12]

The same writer went on to note that it is difficult to tell the difference between Andropov and a Jesuit, especially when the "Jesuit is wearing a red Andropov T shirt."[13] In other words the "leftist" regime is very definitely and very closely intertwined with Roman Catholicism in general and the Jesuits in particular. The guru of the Sandinista revolution is Ernesto Cardenal, a Trappist Monk; the foreign minister is E'Escoto, a Maryknoll priest; and the brains behind the whole operation, Fernando Cardenal, is a Jesuit. When these three "Marxist" Roman Catholic clergymen join forces with the strongman Daniel Ortego, who preaches about a revolutionary being a Christian and vice-versa, it is indeed difficult to escape the blanket of Jesuit casuistry which seems to cover the revolution in Nicaragua.

If we are to believe the New Solidarity paper, which takes a definite Roman Catholic stance, there is not much hope for the liberation of Nicaragua from the hands of the Vatican-Jesuit-connection. For this paper states that the man the U.S. is grooming to replace the Sandinistas, Eden Pastora, who is now building a base of operations in Honduras, is Jesuit-controlled himself. So that even if the Sandinistas were removed tomorrow, another Jesuit-controlled man would be installed, this time with the help of the C.I.A. and the U.S. government.

Where the Jesuits end and the Marxists begin is certainly a difficult question to answer, but one thing is certain as of this writing: the Jesuits are in control of Nicaragua. All the banks of Nicaragua were nationalized when the Sandinistas took over except the Ambriosano Group. This group mysteriously escaped nationalization. The reason being, of course, that the Ambrosiano Group is controlled by the Vatican.

The Vatican has kept the people in Central America in ignorance and misery for four centuries. It is in the interest of the Vatican to keep its stranglehold on these nations. They are doing so either by the death squads in El Salvador or the Jesuit Marxists in Nicaragua, but they are maintaining their hold over the people. The U.S. as a Protestant country could bring some pressure to bear, which could really liberate the people from both warring factions, but alas, no such pressure is ever brought to bear on the Vatican. Instead the U.S. seems to become more and more the lackey of the Vatican, and the power that keeps the rotten status quo in place in Latin America.

A classic example of their failure to uphold the one truly free government in Central America was seen in the case of Rios Montt in Guatamala. Rios Montt was a charismatic Protestant. He had his limitations, to be sure, but he was beginning to bring some real liberty to the people of Guatamala. As far as we can ascertain the Roman Catholic church began to agitate for his removal. We only picked up small items of news here and there, but we did read that some "leaders" in Guatamala were concerned that unless he was removed, he was going to cause a civil war in Guatamala. One item also spoke of the fact that anti-catholic feeling was being generated by his fanatical form of Christianity. (All this is the same old Jesuit line we are seeing in Canada and the U.S. tdoay. That is, no one should say anything against the Pope or Roman Catholicism. As we are typing these pages we read that several people have been arrested in Canada for distributing "anti-catholic" literature. Imagine, if you can, getting arrested in a so-called free country for passing out literature of a theological nature. Truly the freedoms of the Protestant Reformation are being seriously abridged right now in North America.) Montt was deposed, and the Vatican returned to power in Guatamala with the tacit approval of the C.I.A. Protestant Americans better wake up!

The Vatican is the center of a never ending web of conspiracy. It is working day and night to bring the world to the feet of the Roman pontiff. The Vatican octopus has tentacles reaching into almost every government circle on earth. When the Red Chinese needed the off-shore oil drilling expertise of the United States (no other country possesses it) a bargain was struck so that the Jesuits were once again allowed into China. Surely such a move is almost incredible when viewed in the light of the fact that America is still an overwhelmingly Protestant nation at least in the numerical make-up of her population.

The Vatican works incessantly at building bridges over which its plans may be put into operation. Pedro Arrupe, then the head of the Jesuits, was the man that Pope Paul VI sent to Moscow in 1971. He met with the communists to try to get the then repressive government of Czechoslovakia to relax her repressive policies. When he returned from Moscow he stated that he saw signs of relaxation of religious persecution in Russia. (Billy Graham came back with the same line.) Arrupe was immediately challenged by the Director of Lithuanian Catholic Aid, Casimir Pugevicus, who said that Arrupe's statement was a "time serving Soviet maneuver used in order to create a false impression."[14] It is obvious that the Vatican wants a soft line taken toward Communist Russia because the ultimate goal of the one world church envisaged by the Vatican is the total absorption of all into the one true fold of Romanism.

Bible Protestantism is the only faith that can never capitulate to Romanism. Romanism with its ability to absorb false religions into its fold will become the cage of every unclean bird. But it can never absorb Bible Protestantism because the difference between the two is of such a nature that union is spiritually and ecclesiastically impossible. This is the reason biblically ignorant newsmen speak of the bigotry of the bible-believing fundamentalists of our times; they do not realize the eternal difference that exists between vital biblical Christianty on the one hand and all false religions on the other. So Bible Protestantism must ultimately be the target of every conspiracy, and the target of the final apostate conglomerate.

REFERENCES

1. Liddy G. Gordon, *Will,* Dell Publ. Co., 1981, p.54
2. Ibid., p.383
3. *Canadian Revivalist,* Nov./Dec., 1981, p.4
4. *Church and State,* Vol. 28, No. 8, p.3
5. Yallop, David, *IN GOD'S NAME,* Bantam Books, N.Y., N.Y., 1984, p.313
6. Ibid., p.117
7. Ibid., p.X
8. Small, Gretchen, *New Solidarity,* March 8, 1982, p.3
9. loc cit.
10. AP News Release
11. *U.S. NEWS & WORLD REPORT,* Sept. 3, 1984, p.46
12. *New Solidarity,* April 25, 1983, p.6
13. loc cit.
14. Martin, Malachi, *The Final Conclave,* Stein and Day, N.Y., 1978, p.86

A FINANCIAL EMPIRE SECOND TO NONE

Whenever anyone writes on conspiracy money is always given a prominent place. In this regard the Vatican certainly does not take a back seat to anyone. The wealth of the Vatican, as we will see, is so vast that in all probability its true worth will never be known.

We are going to examine in some detail what various writers, who have tried to research the wealth of the Vatican, have said. Several of these writers are members of the Roman Catholic church. It is surely interesting to every Protestant that when Pope Paul brought his entourage from Milan to the Vatican, they were dubbed by Roman Catholic writers as the Milan Mafia.[1]

It is not within the bounds of this study to examine the Mafia in detail. But the Cosa Nostra, the Family, or The Mafia are a 100% Roman Catholic outfit. They originated in Sicily where Michele Sindona was also born. They control vast holdings in Italy and North America. They have gone what they call "legit" in many enterprises and were able to close down an entire cheese plant in Wisconsin. They did this to establish a monopoly in the Pizza business. This incident made the national news. Businessmen came in and brought the cheese factory. After they bought it, they closed it down. It was only later that Mafia involvement was discovered. As far as we know, the factory, which employed most of the town's work force, is still closed down as of this writing.

It is interesting to notice the timing of the move by the Mafia to control the cheese and pizza business in the United States. Panatella, a Vatican controlled company dealing mainly in flour and pasta, lost two and a half million dollars just prior to the Mafia takeover and required financing of 4.8 million dollars to keep it afloat.

Martin discloses that by the late sixties both the Institute for Religious Words (whose assets were conservatively put at 3 billion dollars) and the Special Administration of Holy See Property were invested in every sector of Italian industry and commerce. He went on to say, "On the boards of directors of companies in which the Vatican had an interest there always sat a Vatican ' family ' man, somebody like Massimo Spada or Luigi Mennini."[2]

Martin also pointed out that the Special Administration of Holy See Property, which was run by competent lay bankers, was advised by J. P. Morgan, Hambros Brothers of London, and the Rothschilds of Paris.

Ostling recounts the story of Boys' Town, a Roman Catholic charity.

> Boys Town now has a worth of well over $200 million, including a securities portfolio valued (very conservatively) at $157 million. Although the interest on such a nest egg is ample to operate the Town, it still spends millions to send the traditional tearjerker fund appeals to 34 million people and raises nearly $18 million a year. This means Boys Town has about three times the endowment of Notre Dame University, raises more money than the Greater New York United Fund, and would rank 372nd in assets on the Fortune 500 if if were a business corporation. All this for 700 boys.[3]

All this came to light after much digging by a weekly newspaper in Omaha, Nebraska.

According to Lo Bello, a Roman Catholic journalist, the Vatican is the only sovereign state that never publishes a budget. He was accused of exaggeration in his estimates of Vatican wealth, but suffice it to say, the wealth of the Vatican must be immense, for a simple honest disclosure of its holdings, if they do not constitute great wealth, would lay to rest all the "extravagant" estimates of various writers, but such a disclosure has not been forthcoming.

The Sindona debacle, which the Vatican sought to hide from the general public, resulted in a loss of close to one billion dollars. Yet the Vatican carried on as before, demonstrating its reservoir of financial reserves as nothing else could. Very few companies could sustain such a loss and carry on without so much as a whisper. (Chrysler Corporation lost half a billion and would have gone under but for the U. S. government.)

The financial tentacles of the Vatican reach into numerous banks in different countries. Yallop says that the Rothschilds in Paris have been doing business with the Vatican since early in the 19th century.[4] He goes on to point out that, "Credit Suisse, Hambros, Morgan Guaranty, Bankers Trust, Chase Manhattan, and Continental Illinois among others became Vatican partners."[5]

This financial empire which finances the Vatican conspiracy is filled with murder and mayhem. Yallop states, "The murder of Luciano-Pope John Paul I was to stop him from removing Marcinkus who was the foundation holding up Calvi, Sindona, and Celli."[6] When the dust had cleared from John Paul's mysterious death, it left in its aftermath a series of murders, assassinations and "suicides" that only the Mafia could match for cold bloodedness. Of the main players in the scene only Marcinkus and Celli still remain in control. Yallop recounts in detail each one of the murders and "suicides," and his pages, which are very difficult to refute, make grim reading. His book, *IN GOD'S NAME*," merits close reading by all who are concerned about freedom.

Because of the criticism that no disclosure is ever made of its wealth, the Vatican has in recent years tried to reform some of its monetary policies, but much still remains to be done. No estimate can be given of the immense wealth of the Vatican, but one can get some glimpses of the multi-billion dollar enterprise through various works that have appeared in recent years.

Ostling, in his work, *"Secrecy in The Church,"* written from the standpoint of one sympathetic to the Church, does give some interesting insights into the wealth of the Papacy.

He recounts that the late Bishop James A. Pike (a convert from Romanism to Episcopalianism) wrote what he calls a sensational article in which he said that the Jesuits had a controlling interest in the Bank of America, the nation's largest, and that they earned 250 million dollars a year from their investments (a quarter of a billion). He goes on to say that the Jesuits "sputtered, but they have never made a full accounting of their holdings."[7] Gollin, a freelance writer who tried to research Papal wealth, figured the securities and commercial properties of the Dioceses of the U.S. at almost "one billion dollars."[8] Nino Lo Bello put "the American Jesuit's annual income at $250 million." He claims that all Catholic units in the U.S. and Canada combined have assets of more than $80 billion and an annual income of nearly $12.5 billion."[9]

It was none other than Cardinal Vagnozzi who observed concerning the Vatican's finances:

It would take a combination of the KGB, the C.I.A. and Interpol to obtain just an inkling of how much and where the monies are.[10]

According to this Cardinal three of the most powerful agencies in the world could only obtain an inkling of how much the Vatican is worth. Yallop points out that the "Vatican bought into General Motors, Shell, Gulf Oil, General Electric, Bethlehem Steel, IBM and TWA." He went on to say that "the Vicar of Christ had acquired a new unofficial title: Chairman of the Board."[11]

The Vatican also acquired "controlling interest in companies, in fields of insurance, steel, financing, flour and spaghetti, industry, cement and real estate."[12] It owns sections of downtown Montreal, Canada, sections of Mexico City in Mexico, many of the major hotels in Italy, blocks of real estate on the Champs D'Elysee in Paris, the Watergate area in Washington, D.C., real estate in New York City, and the entire satellite city of Lomas Verdes in Mexico. This is only the tip of the iceberg, for much of the Vatican's wealth is hidden in holding companies so that it is difficult to come even close in an estimate of its vast wealth. It is interesting to observe also that Pope John Paul, who was murdered in the Vatican, intended to reform the Vatican's finances. Yallop in his work claims that this could have been one of a half dozen reasons why he was murdered right in the Vatican. Another very interesting fact is that Pope John Paul confessed to Father Dezza. Even the Pope has a prelate to whom he confesses, and poor Pope John Paul for some reason chose the head of the Jesuits as his "Father Confessor." If for any reason he chose to confide some of his proposed changes to Dezza, he may have unwittingly sealed his own death warrant.

Malachi Martin, former Jesuit professor at the Pontifical Biblical Institute in Rome, in his new book, *"RICH CHURCH POOR CHURCH,"* puts the wealth of the "church" at 300 billion dollars. He points out that the Vatican is the:

> largest single stockholder in the world with about $20 billion dollars traceably invested (but much more untraceably invested) with gold deposits exceeding those of most medium sized countries, and with a worldwide real estate operation.[13]

He goes on to say in another place:

> a list of the companies and banks in Italy and abroad in which

the Vatican acquired a controlling interest before the out-
break of World War II, when added to the list of those in which
it acquired a minor but substantial interest, would fill some
sixty or seventy pages of this book.[14]

Even Martin, who still classes himself as a Roman Catholic, is
appalled at the extent of the Vatican's wealth when contrasted
with the impoverished millions of Roman Catholics around the
world. The present Pope speaks much about economic justice
Although much has been written about the present Pope in
glowing terms, Yallop does not share the international newsmen's
accolade. Yallop states candidly:

> the papacy of John Paul II has been a case of business as
> usual. The business has benefitted immeasurably not only
> from the murder of Albino Luciana, but also from the mur-
> ders that have followed that strange lonely death in the
> Vatican.[15]

He goes on to say:

> Many millions of words have been written since the election
> of Karol Wojtyla in attempts to analyze and understand what
> kind of man he is. As can be seen, he is the kind of man who
> could allow men like Villot, Cody, Marcinkus, Mennini, De
> Strobel and Poletto to remain in office. [16]

He adds:

> "It is a papacy of double standards, one for the Pope and
> one for the rest of mankind.
> "There can be no defense on the grounds of ignorance,
> Marcinkus is directly answerable to the Pope."[17]

REFERENCES

1. Martin, Malachi, *THE FINAL CONCLAVE,* Stein and Day, New York, 1978. p. 18
2. Ibid., p. 26
3. Ostling, Richard, *SECRECY IN THE CHURCH,* Harper and Row, N.Y. 1974, p. 51
4. Yallop, David, *IN GOD'S NAME,* Bantam Books, N.Y., N.Y. 1984, p 97
5. loc. cit.
6. Ibid., p. 103
7. Ostling, p. 49
8. loc.cit.
9. Ibid., p. 50
10. Yallop, p. 105
11. Ibid., p. 99
12. Ibid., p. 98
13. Martin, Malachi, *RICH CHURCH POOR CHURCH,* G. P. Putnam's Sons, N.Y., N.Y. 1984, p. 14
14. Ibid., p. 40
15. Yallop, p. 264
16. Ibid, p. 265
17. Ibid., p. 264

THE CONSPIRACY OF MISDIRECTION

Satan has a plan for this world. His plan is doomed to failure, but that does not mean it is to be taken lightly or that it cannot affect men and nations and do untold harm before it is finally frustrated.

Dr. Stuart McBirnie retraced the steps of the Apostle Paul's missionary journeys. In those cities where the great Apostle had established churches in the first century, the cause of Christianity has disappeared. McBirnie recounted how not only was he not able to find a church of any kind, but in some instances he could not even find one Christian. So although the gates of Hell will not prevail against the Church of the Living Christ, some local churches do fold up and disappear under the onslaught of the devil and this world.

Satan has been at work since the fall of man. So his Satanic conspiracy to dominate this world is of age long duration. Satan's primary area of operation we saw in our first study as the area of religion. Only God's believing remnant can understand this aspect of the conspiracy, and even many of them are at sea at this point. Every unsaved person thinks that religion is a good thing when in fact only vital biblical Christianity is a good thing: every other religion is a satanic counterfeit. Satan is working to deceive the nations. He works through individuals. It should be obvious to every thinking person that there are people working day and night to overthrow vital biblical Christianity and many of these individuals are religious, even posing as "Christians." In other words the battle we face is primarily a spiritual one. It will not be defeated by merely legal efforts or even protests unless the protests are centered on a proper interpretation of the Word of God.

Romanism has made unbelievable advances in the United States in the last one hundred years. As one leading Roman Catholic spokesman said, "We are less than one hundred years from Rum, Romanism and Rebellion, referring to the slogan of American politicians at the close of the nineteenth century. (See our first booklet for further documentation.)

Gary Allen in his examination of conspiracy fails to come to grips with known historical conspiracies. For one reason or another he obviously ignores the documented religious conspiracies of history. Roman Catholic conspiracies are part of the historical record. Papal plots have been discovered, and the conspirators arrested and brought to trial at various junctures of history. Father Chiniquy portrays Romanists as the main plotters in the assassination of Abraham Lincoln. So the Vatican has been working night and day to shift the burden of conspiracy from its shoulders to some other group of conspirators. Since the McCarthy era, extremist groups have painted almost every leader in the United States as Communist, pro-communist, or an insider. NO ONE HAS EVER LOOKED AT THE PAPAL INTRIGUE, which is still going on today as it has for over 1,000 years. While men hunt for shadowy conspirators among America's leaders, who evidence no continuity whatsoever, Romanism, with a continuity in conspiracy unparalleled in the history of man, continues to flourish and to call the shots in the area of religion and politics.

It should be obvious to every Bible-believer that one of the main tasks of the Satanic conspiracy is to direct those who are seeking to discover the conspiracy and alert Christians to it to some other apparent culprit. This we term the conspiracy of misdirection. Misdirection is written large in the field of conspiracy.

We see this conspiracy of misdirection focused in four main areas.

1. Toward the Masons

The Masons have become a favorite whipping boy for conspiratorialists writing on the great global conspiracy. While we do not approve of the Masons, we do not believe the Roman Catholic propaganda put out against the Masons. Yallop postulates a secret Masonic Conspiracy against the Vatican in his work, *"IN GOD'S NAME."* Michele Sindona is also linked to the Masons by Yallop, Martin, and other writers. Sindona came out of Sicily, the reputed home of the Mafia but is regarded as a Mason by Martin. He is certainly a man of mystery. But to try to link him to the Masonic Lodge and hint at some hidden conspiracy by the Masons to destroy the Roman Catholic Church through financial embezzlement is more fiction than fact. It is true that Sindona was linked to the loss of almost one billion dollars, which the Vatican financial empire sustained, and that he at one time was a close friend of Pope Paul. According to Newsweek he was the brains behind

> an intricate group of holding companies (and) he controlled a chain of hotels, a giant multinational real-estate operation, several industrial firms in Europe and America, half a dozen banks. Rumor had it that he was the Pope's chief financial adviser, or alternatively, the Mafia's number one banker.[1]

When Pope Paul realized the amount of money involved in the Sindona scandal, he said that Sindona was in the "hands of unknown powers," hinting at some dark super-conspiracy against the Papacy. For it is a belief of many Roman Catholics and even some "Protestant" writers, that the great conspiracy is not directed by Rome but is directed at Rome. At least Malachi Martin seems to indicate as much in his work. He tells that:

> Montini (who later became Pope Paul) had known that over in the Quirinal...and within the Vatican behind Pacelli's back, there were men and women who dealt every day in millions of church dollars —the "Patrimony of St. Peter"— buying war and selling peace down the river, cynically scandalously....Montini could almost see a Satanic rictus behind the whole affair.[2]

Martin also points out that late in the Sindona scandal, "It is now reported to Paul that Michele Sindona is a member of the Masonic order."[3] Before the whole affair with Sindona was over, Paul was to feel that Sindona was a shadowy figure behind some great conspiracy against the Papacy.

Roman Catholic writers, of course, do not believe in a Roman Catholic conspiracy. So they are constantly proffering Masonry or some other Bilderberger or Tri-lateralist conspiracy as the real one. Some conservative Protestants, who do not know their Bibles, have taken up the cry of the Roman Catholic conspiratorialists. But to try to link Michele Sindona to some conspiracy against the papacy is a difficult task. For the few things that we do know about his early education show that he was educated by the Jesuits. Also his bank failures, while definitely affecting the Vatican, also affected him. The Vatican not only lost millions, but Michele Sindona lost so much that he was wiped out. So if Sindona was in the hands of "unknown powers," they must have been unknown to him too, for they certainly deserted him when he needed a friend. The powers, which seem to be connected with Sindona, were the Mafia. For the main government witness against him, Giorgio Ambroscoli, who had been appointed to liquidate the Sindona controlled banks in Italy, was killed in Milan. No one was ever charged with the crime.

Sindona had to flee to America where after another bank failure he was arrested and brought to trial and sentenced to five years on "65 counts of conspiracy, fraud and perjury."[4] The truth that must be grasped in this whole Sindona scenario is that Sindona, who drew a lot of attention to the Vatican, is now out of commission and thoroughly discredited. But the Vatican is still there, directing would-be conspiracy hunters away from the Vatican conspiracy to Insider, Bilderberger or other shadowy conspiracies. The enduring nature of the Vatican power base makes it a prime suspect in the field of conspiracy.

Michele Sindona was at one time one of the most powerful men in Italy. He was also closely identified with Vatican finances. It seems to us that there is much more substance to the assertion that Sindona was probably "done in" by the Vatican instead of vice-versa. Sindona was about to be investigated by the Italian government. The man sent to investigate his bank, who unearthed many things, some of them probably not complimentary to the Vatican, was murdered for his trouble. Yallop believes that he was murdered by the Mafia. However it appears obvious that Sindona had now become a very possible international embarrassment to the Vatican, and he himself maintained that he fled to the United states to escape being murdered.

After arriving here, even the bank that he owned in the United States went under. Again the only power on earth able to bring banks down in any one of fifty countries is the Vatican. It not only wields great financial clout but has hundreds of dedicated devotees in powerful positions in banks and financial institutions, which it does not even control, to help fulfil its plans. Sindona went down, down, down without a friend to help. His financial fortune for the most part disappeared almost over night. Yallop believes that Sindona is a suspect behind the murder of Pope John Paul I. It seems that Sindona for all his mystery really had little or no clout at all in the end. He just went to jail. As Hammer points out in his book, *"THE VATICAN CONNECTION,"* the Roman Catholic New York policeman, who linked the Vatican to the Mafia and to a billion dollar counterfeit scam, when nothing was ever done to bring the culprits to justice, said he had finally realized that if you are powerful enough, you are beyond the reach of the law. Sindona was not that powerful!

Hammer says of Coffey, the New York Irish American Roman Catholic policeman, who had tracked the links of the Mafia right into the heart of the Vatican in a billion dollar counterfeit scheme so vast that few would believe it:

> There had been months of plodding along twisted and tangled pathways that seemed to be leading nowhere, and moments of startling breakthrough and discovery...Often during those years as the scope of the hunt and its consequence became clear, he had been convinced that this was what he had been born to do, that this would be the capstone of his career. And now it was over, ended not with the glittering victories he had foreseen but on a sour and cynical note. HE COULD NO LONGER DENY WHAT HE HAD NOT WANTED TO BELIEVE: THERE ARE PEOPLE SO POWERFUL AND SO HIGHLY PLACED THAT THEY ARE IMPERVIOUS TO THE LAW, AND THAT SOCIETY'S RULES AND CODES DO NOT APPLY TO THEM.[5] (emphasis ours)

The main lesson that Hammer's book teaches is that it is easier to bring down the President of the United States than a crook in the Vatican.

When the investigation ended, Aronwald, who was testifying before a Senate sub-committee in Washington said:

> Because of serious allegations that had been made with respect to someone in the Vatican although the name of the individual was never given, the Department of Justice made contacts with the Vatican and obtained their cooperation... As a result of our visit and a result of the cooperation of the Vatican, we were able to conclude that there was no substance to the allegation that anyone within the Vatican was culpably involved in this scheme.[6]

In other words, there was a complete whitewash of the whole investigation. So while the real criminals go free, lesser men are prosecuted and sent to jail. Michele Sindona was one of the ones who went to jail. So although a financial wizard, in some ways he proved to be quite vulnerable in the end while the Vatican men roll on without batting an eye, cleared of all culpability.

The charges against Sindona were also the same as those made against Nogara, the financial wizard who put the Vatican on the map financially. Nogara was the brains behind the reorganization of the whole financial structure of the Vatican in 1929. He succeeded in moving the Vatican fortunes from millions to billions before he retired in 1958. However, he was investigated on the charges that he was a Mason and belonged to a secret masonic society and was secretly conspiring against the Vatican. The same old story trotted out against Sindona and also written large in modern books dealing with Conspiracy. (See Yallop, Allen, and Bowen for corroboration.)

Not only was Nogara not a Masonic man, nor a conspirator against the "church," he was one of the most loyal hard working sons of the "church" that Italy ever produced. Not only was he not out to ruin the Vatican, he helped it on to such financial success that it now has become one of the richest organizations on earth. When the investigation was completed by the Vatican loyalists, the taciturn Nogara was completely exonerated of all charges against him, and the record showed that he was completely trustworthy, a loyal son of the Vatican in every respect. Yet these rumors and charges persist in every generation and are still being made today.

We believe that the reason we hear of "secret Masonic conspiracies" is to keep the idea of a mock conspiracy before the people to keep them from seeing the real thing. These writers lack one thing in their writings on conspiracy, and that is an in-depth exegesis of Revelation 17-18. They focus attention on the Masons to draw away attention from the Vatican and to create sympathy for the Pope and Papacy, who are then considered victims of the conspiracy rather than the brains behind it.

2. The second theory that we see written large in contemporary works is the Insider theory. That is, that a certain group of financiers are at work to control the world. Gary Allen, of course, postulates this idea as do others like William Bowen. Allen states:

In the Bolshevik Revolution we have some of the world's richest and most powerful men financing a movement which claims its very existence is based upon the concept of stripping of their wealth men like the Rothschilds, Rockefellers, Schiffs, Warburgs, Morgans, and Harrimans, and Milners. But obviously these men have no fear of international communism. It is only to assume that if they financed it and do not fear it, it must be because they control it.... Remember that for 150 years it has been standard operating procedure of the Rothschilds and their allies to control both sides of every conflict.[7]

It certainly is easy to direct attention toward the Rothschilds because of their great wealth and also because they are Jews. What Allen fails to see is that every accusation that can be made against the Rothschilds and their allies can also be made against the Vatican with much more weight. The Rothschilds' wealth, although immense, is not in the same league with the Vatican's. The tentacles of the Rothschilds do not reach into every government on earth with anything approaching the same degree as the Vatican's. The longevity of the alleged conspiracy of the Rothschilds, according to Allen himself, goes back a mere 150 years—again nothing in comparison to the Papacy whose global ambitions and intrigue go back more than a thousand years.

Again the idea of operating on both sides of every major conflict with which Allen charges the Rothschilds can be seen in the history of Vatican power politics with far greater documentation to support it. It can even be seen right now in Central America at this very moment. The Vatican is on both sides in El Salvador and Nicaragua, and the intrigue of the Jesuits on both sides of the conflicts is causing such an uproar that the Pope traveled there to try to defuse the embarrassing situation.

3. The third idea of the conspiracy that faces America is "Secular humanism." William Bowen in his book, "GLOBALISM-AMERICA'S DEMISE," spends much time and effort trying to pin America's troubles on the secular humanists. This has become a popular theme with other conservative writers as well. We would be the last to downplay the effect that secular humanism has had on America, but we do not think that secular humanism is the global conspiracy that confronts the world.

In fact we believe that the flurry over secular humanism at the present time is another case of misdirection. The real conspiracy is much more closely knit and has much clearer goals. The drift of America from her Protestant moorings allows the religious men to take over. We get tired of listening to those who speak of America's Judeo-Christian ethic. America was founded upon historic Bible Protestantism. Anyone who has studied early American history knows that her people were made up of the persecuted Protestants of Europe who fled here for a refuge and built the greatest country the world has ever seen. It was built solidly on English-Puritanism, Scottish Presbyterianism, Scots-Irish-Presbyterianism, German Pietism and Dutch Calvinism. As for Jews and Roman Catholics, they were almost unheard of in the early days of America. And they certainly had little or no influence outside Rhode Island and Maryland. Why do we never hear of this in any of the writings which conservatives write today? You would think that American liberties came from the Jews and Roman Catholics. America is going down because the Protestant Puritan ethic upon which she was founded is being replaced not by a secular humanism but by an effete false religion which will not mention the past but will praise the Roman anti-christ. This is the crux of America's trouble. God judges idolatry whether our half-baked modern Protestant Christian writers realize it or not. America is going down not from secular humanism nor a false pietism but from a love affair with idolatry and false religion.

It is indeed very strange that we hear nothing about the Inquisition today. In reading the *"STEALING OF AMERICA,"* we note that the secular humanists are the ones we have to fear. When illustrations are drawn of persecutions in the past, mention is made of the early Christians, who were thrown to the lions in the Roman arena and of Christians, who were tortured under Communism in Eastern Europe.

Various philosophers are named in recent books as the cause of the downfall of western civilization. In all this plethora of writing about the demise of America because of certain sinister forces, no mention is ever made of the Inquisition which lasted 500 years. Is that not passing strange?

We hear of the Hordes of the French Revolution but not the Massacre of St. Bartholmew's Day, carried out not by atheists, secular humanists or a totalitarian state, but by those claiming to be religious and belonging to the only true "church." Secular humanism is made out to be the unstoppable force while Romanism flourishes in America as never before. While misguided Protestants stare at "Secular Humanism," Romanism controls the White House, the C.I.A., the F.B.I., the Congress, and most of the leading posts in the present Reagan Administration.

Manhattan observes:

> The existence of such an organically oriented Catholic body would have been a matter of concern itself, but the fact that it enjoyed the patronage of the most eminent individuals of the U.S. political intelligence and military establishment, made their presence one of profound disquiet. The list, although minimal, was impressive: from General Alexander Haig, Secretary of State, (since deposed) to Mr. Casey, head of the Central Intelligence Agency; from D. Regan of the U.S. Treasury to Mr. Allen of the National Security; from Mrs. Kirkpatrick, UNO, to W. Clark, who replaced Allen in 1982, to W.S. Wilson, the U.S. envoy at the Vatican and a convert to Catholicism, and many others in less glamorous but nonetheless very influencial posts up and down the administration.[8]

As of this writing President Reagan has appointed an ambassador to the Vatican, and he has pledged that if reelected he would fight for the family in the spirit of Pope John Paul II. So Vatican influence is written large in American politics today. (As for fighting for the family, the papacy has been the greatest enemy of the family in most Roman Catholic countries in the world, grinding the family under its tyrannical heel all over Central America, South America, Southern Europe, Eire, and wherever it has been entrenched for centuries.)

The blackout which has been thrown over the Inquisition and the massacres and persecutions of Romanism apparently is no accident. Conservative writers apparently believe that the United States has nothing to fear from the Vatican, and therefore, they seem to have tacitly agreed not to mention known historical horrors connected with Rome's global ambitions.

The use of the word "Christian" today by many of these writers, who would alert us to the evils that confront us, is obviously an omnibus term. It obviously includes in its meaning, as used today, the unchristian religion of Romanism.

So in saving America from the secular humanist conspiracy, we are being herded along with Romanism to do the job. Such writing leaves a lot to be desired as far as the Biblical Christian is concerned. One has only to look at a nation where Romanism holds absolute sway to see that the Vatican can match anything any secular state has ever produced in the way of suppression and more.

Biblical Christians, keep to your Bibles! Do not be misled even by sincere men, who have not done their homework in church history nor apparently in Bible Doctrine.

4. The fourth idea put forward to misdirect us concerning the Global Conspiracy is the Usurper Theory. This theory links the Vatican to the conspiracy but maintains that the Pope is kidnapped or killed and his place taken by another man who is a Communist or atheist.

The idea is written large in contemporary works although it is not new. The Novel, *"THE JANUS POPE,"* is a story about the real pope being kidnapped and a Communist put in his place. Although this book has some of the characters saying nasty things about the Vatican, the idea that the Pope is God's representative or God's deputy is put forward a number of times. So the author apparently views the pope as Christ's vicar upon earth.

Malachi Martin in his book, *"THE FINAL CONCLAVE,"* also alludes to this idea of usurpation. The national news media also gave large coverage to the Bulgarian Connection in their attempts to assassinate the Pope. So that the impression is given to the unthinking that the real conspiracy, even though it does involve the papacy, involves it only as the target of the intrigue and not as the originator of it.

Dean Alford in his *"PROLEGOMENA TO THE REVELATION"* points out that even Roman Catholic expositors see the papacy in Revelation 17 and 18.

From Joachim's time...men's mind even WITHIN THE ROMISH CHURCH, became accustomed to the idea that the apocalyptic Babylon was in some sense or other not only Pagan but PAPAL ROME; and that Antichrist was to sit, whether as an usurper or not, on the throne of the papacy.[9] (emphasis ours)

Joachim was Abbot of Flores in the 12th Century. He denounced even back then the corruption of the Roman clergy, the issue of indulgences, the deification of the Roman Church and the Crusades. He saw in the Revelation the description of the Papacy as Mystery Babylon the Great and the Mother of Harlot religion.

So with such a crushing weight to dispose of, it is not surprising that the idea of a usurper upon the seat of the papacy is written large in contemporary thought. Something had to be done to offset Protestant suspicions of a secret cabal in the heart of the Vatican. So a massive propaganda effort to educate Protestants in the niceties of the papacy and the evil machinations of some other shadowy conspirators out to destroy this nice institution had to be launched. The sad thing is that apparently millions of Protestants have bought this idea without even a second thought. Malachi Martin, a former Jesuit, may still imagine that there are many Protestants who believe in this secret cabal in the heart of the Vatican, but in actuality their number is very, very small. By far the majority of modern Protestants have swallowed the Vatican line.

REFERENCES

1. Newsweek, Aug. 20, 1979, p. 67
2. Martin, *THE FINAL CONCLAVE*, p. 29
3. Ibid., p. 64
4. Time, April 7, 1980, p. 59
5. Hammer, Richard, *THE VATICAN CONNECTION*, Charter Books, N.Y. 1982, p. 309
6. Ibid., p. 308
7. Allen, Gary, *NONE DARE CALL IT CONSPIRACY*, Concord Press, Rossmoor, California 1971, pp 73-75
8. Manhattan, Avro, *THE VATICAN-WASHINGTON, MOSCOW ALLIANCE*, Chick Pub., 1982, p. 65
9. Alford, Henry, *THE GREEK NEW TESTAMENT*, Vol. VI, Guardian Press, Grand Rapids, Mich. 1976., Reprint, p. 246

CONCLUDING REMARKS

Malachi Martin says:

> For too long now those in the higher echelons of the
> Church have been suspected of quite worldly aims: of secret-
> almost cabalistic-designs on the rights, liberties, and
> freedoms of ordinary people. Many a sincere modern Protes-
> tant is still convinced that this is true.[1]

Martin was a former Jesuit professor. He seems to write from a
very open view point. But in his serious and even severe criti-
cisms of the Vatican in his books, "THE RISE AND FALL OF THE
ROMAN CHURCH," and "RICH CHURCH POOR CHURCH," he
never once criticizes the entity itself. Only things about it, bad
things to be sure, but not the historical reality—and to him—the
true and only church in all of history. Martin is very shrewd. His
open criticism of the church establishes him in the minds of
millions as an enemy of the church. He is far from it. But the idea
that he is a critical enemy gives much more weight to his writings
in the eyes of Protestants, thus enabling him to still latently push
the idea of the Pope as Christ's Vicar upon earth and the Roman
Catholic Church, the only true church that exists.

His contention that many a sincere modern Protestant still is
convinced that there is a cabal, an intrigue by a few powerful men
to take over the world, and that they are centered in the Vatican, is
probably less true now than at any point in Protestant history. We
would have to say that VERY FEW modern Protestants even view
the Papacy as other than another denomination, and even fewer
still see anything even approaching cabalistic designs on the part
of its leaders as the foregoing pages demonstrate. The powerful
impact of papal propaganda is beginning to show itself together
with the almost total apathy and indifference of most modern
Protestants to Bible Interpretation. The complete failure of
anything even approaching a Protestant solidarity against the obvious encroachments of papal teachings in once Protestant
America proves the truth of the foregoing sentences.

The complete ignorance and apathy of most American Protestants to the Vatican designs on America is, to say the least, disturbing. Not only that, but even those, who are supposed to be informed and even write books to warn Americans about the dangers which this nation faces, never even mention Romanism much less examine its goals for America.

We hear much about perversion today and of how America will go down the tubes if the "Gays" have their way. But no one ever mentions doctrinal perversion. Doctrinal perversion is always the forerunner of sexual perversion. The Scriptures are clear at this point. "Even as they did not like to retain God in their knowledge God gave them over unto a reprobate mind to do those things which are not convenient." The Scriptures teach clearly that the wrath of God is revealed from heaven against those who hold back the truth in unrighteousness. Doctrinal perversion leads to idolatry which leads to sexual perversion according to Romans Chapter one.

When the Pope of Rome preaches the perverted doctrines of Romanism, enforced celibacy, purgatory, Mariolatry, etc., he is as much a threat to a pure America as any sexual pervert who clamours for "Gay" rights. This is the truth that we must see today or perish as a nation. Impure doctrines of demons affect a society more than the impure actions of some of its members.

The nature of our battle is spiritual. When the Biblical truths of the Word of God with which evil is defeated are replaced by the satanic drivel of false religion, that society which experiences the barrage of satanic drivel is every bit as bad off as any secular humanist society. Secular humanism is not the only evil facing North America! In fact, North America has far more to fear from religious idolatry than it has from secular humanists.

Jerry Falwell, Billy Graham, Francis Schaeffer and Ronald Reagan are all working to defeat the secular humanists. But none of them even has one word to say about the religious idolatry which curses America. Apparently, it is all right for that to flourish. In other words as long as a person can say he is religious, he is not considered a threat to the freedoms that many Americans still hold dear.

We would have to say candidly; the judgment of God has a far greater chance of falling upon America because of idolatrous false religion than it does because of secular humanism. We oppose the atheistic humanists without reservation, but we do not believe that this is where the heat of the battle rages in America today. We believe that America's love affair with the Great Whore who sits on the Tiber poses a far greater threat to America's freedoms than any other evil which America faces today.

We recognize the power of Communism. We recognize the power of Islam. We recognize the power of secular humanism. We also recognize the power of Romanism; and we would have to say that a candid look at America today will show that of the four evils mentioned, Romanism constitutes by far the biggest internal threat to America today than any of the others.

As America becomes more and more idolatrous, she comes more and more under the indictment of the Second Commandment. God's wrath is repeatedly poured out in the Scriptures upon his chosen people for their idolatry. (This sin is never mentioned once by most modern writers.) In the second commandment, which is not taught in Roman Catholic schools, God is spoken of as "visiting the iniquity of the fathers unto the third and fourth generation of them that hate me," a fearful judgment which our modern writers never mention and perhaps do not even believe is actual. This judgmental visitation of God upon succeeding generations is because of IDOLATRY, not atheism nor pornography.

It is great to make accusations against the Bilderbergers and the Insiders and the Illuminati because almost everyone in the world can identify against such people. The very capability of being able to identify against them, we believe, points up the weakness in such accusations. According to the Word of God, which is supposed to be the final authority for Bible Protestants, when false Christs and false prophets arise, the only ones who are not deceived are God's elect people. In other words, as we pointed out in our first booklet, this world of people will go along with false religion, the rise of Mystery Babylon the Great, and will worship the Anti-Christ.

It is only God's elect people who will in every generation stand against the encroachments of religious evil. So if the evil is so identified that most of the world can be antagonistic toward it, it is in all probability not the beginning, middle or end of the final apostate conglomerate, which is to rule the earth and be the cage of EVERY UNCLEAN bird.

The Vatican has been the center of evil and uncleanness now

for more than a thousand years. It was the Mother of the Inquisition which tortured, persecuted and martyred multiplied millions of precious believers for 500 years. Wilder states in his careful study:

> that the records of historians and martyrologists show that it may be reasonable to estimate that from fifty to sixty-eight millions of human beings died, suffered torture, lost their possessions, or were otherwise devoured by the Roman Catholic Church during the awful years of the Inquisition.[2]

According to Llorente, the official recorder for the Inquisition, until he became absolutely revulsed by it, more than 300,000 victims were immolated on the flaming faggots of the Spanish Inquisition alone.[3] It has been the effort of modern Roman Catholic writers to try to play down the Inquisition and to deny its holocaust. But there are many reputable historians, who recount its atrocities for those interested in finding out the truth.

We have a two volume set which deals with the Spanish Inquisitors in Holland. The pages are filled with account after account of torture and horror that would make our ears tingle. It tells of one man who opposed the false doctrines of Rome, who was put on a spit and slowly roasted over an open fire.[4]

The Vatican not only has been the center of cruelty and persecution, it has also been the center of a never ending spate of false doctrine and practice, which if the Bible is true, will lead most of its adherents to a lost eternity. So that the true Bible believer, who is interested in the salvation of souls from sin and from eternal death, is impelled to stand against this onslaught and to warn those caught up in it.

The fact that the Vatican is evil is, of course, admitted by some Roman Catholic writers. They go into great detail in highlighting some of its ancient and modern evils. But the bottom line is that the Roman Catholic Church is the only true church in spite of the evils of the Inquisition, the persecutions of the past, and even the heinous crimes of some of the popes. Malachi Martin criticizes the church severely. But one must be wary in reading such writings.

When Martin criticizes the Vatican, he is criticizing its financial and secular dealings. He is not criticizing its doctrines and teachings. He points out in his book on the decline of the church that it started to decline when it received all the money and land, etc. from Constantine; from then on a struggle developed between its spiritual mission and mammon. He even has in his latest books ideas on how the church is to rid itself of its financial empire, but what he fails to say is that there is to be no revision of nor ridding itself of, its erroneous dogmas and teachings. This is the crux of the whole matter.

To the Bible believing Protestant even if the Roman Catholic Church divested itself of every dime (something that will never happen if Revelation 17 and 18 are true) it would still be a reservoir of evil and error. Its unscriptural teaching on Purgatory is a producer of great evil in several ways. It makes people believe they can buy their way out of trouble in the hereafter, thus affecting everything they do in this life. It also deceives them as to the true nature of eternity so that those who die expecting to buy their way out of purgatory will instead be lost forever in the lake of fire with no hope of ever being released.

The unscriptural teaching inherent in the Mass is also a producer of great evil. Millions live any old way but believe that by taking a consecrated wafer from the hands of sinful man, they are receiving Christ. The Reformers, Puritans, and early Methodists called the Mass a blasphemous fable. They did not do this to be nasty. They did it because they believed that a proper interpretation of the Scriptures proved that Christ died once for all and his once for all offering never needed to be repeated, for it was final, full, and sufficient to deal with the problem of man's sin. No other offering was needed, and so no other could ever be offered especially by sinful men. The idea that sinful men could offer a sacrifice for sins they rightly believed constituted blasphemy. The reason they called it a fable was also established from Scripture. "This is my body" is obviously a figure of speech and not to be taken literally. Even as the cup, which is the New Testament in my blood, is also a similar figure. No one ever argues for the actual cup being the New Testament although thousands have engaged in the controversy over the elements.

It is a fable to assume that by the magic of a priest the bread actually becomes the actual body of Christ. It is an egregious fable to say the least. Yet this blasphemous fable is foisted upon an unsuspecting Protestant populace almost nightly especially when the Pope goes anywhere in the world today.

The unscriptural teaching of an enforced celibacy is also pushed upon us until we almost vomit. As we write these words, the Pope is visiting Canada. We get his face on every television news program and his speeches in every newspaper. In the Altoona Mirror, September 10, 1984, we were told this about the Pope in Canada.

> John Paul began his twelve day tour of Canada on Sunday and followed his custom of getting straight to the point on controversial religious issues by reaffirming the Catholic (the writer obviously means Roman Catholic, and there is an eternal difference) Church's stand that priests and nuns must never marry.

Three things need to be said about this statement.

1. The Bible says that an enforced celibacy is a doctrine of demons. I Timothy 4:1-3.

> Now the Spirit speaks expressly that in the latter times some shall depart from the faith, giving heed to seducing spirits, and doctrines of demons; speaking lies in hypocrisy having their conscience seared with a hot iron; FORBIDDING TO MARRY....

So according to the Bible those who forbid others to marry are
a.   departed from the faith.
b.   heeding seducing spirits
c.   teaching doctrines of demons
d.   speaking lies
e.   in hypocrisy (not only lies you see but hypocritical ones)
f.   having their conscience seared with a hot iron.

What a devasting indictment from God's inspired, infallible, inerrant and authoritative Word!

2.   Notice it is all right for the Pope to go right to the point on controversial religious issues. Let any Protestant such as Ian Paisley, do the same thing, and he is immediately called a preacher of sectarianism, an arch-bigot or worse. Nobody calls the Pope an arch bigot, or Preacher of Sectarianism, even though he comes out with some of the most bigoted sectarian statements

that ever appear in our modern newspapers.

3. Just a few months ago seven Roman Catholic priests were involved in a sexual scandal with a young woman in California. News about the incident was sketchy as anything detrimental to Rome's good image seldom is considered newsworthy. However, we did learn the following facts. The young woman wanted to be a nun. She met with these priests who seduced her. She finally gave birth to a baby in the Philippines where the priests had sent her on the pretext that she was there studying. They had promised her money. When the money failed to come, she filed a paternity suit against the seven since they all apparently were involved with her. The filing of the suit is what brought the story into the news. We never heard another thing about it except that the Roman Catholic spokesman in Los Angeles intimated that the girl was of low morals and that was why she got the priests involved with her. This resulted in a second suit filed by the girl for defamation of character. She maintained that she was perfectly innocent of the charges and that she went at the start to be a nun in good faith and that the reason she submitted to all seven was because she was under their authority. So much for enforced celibacy! It is indeed a doctrine of demons and the producer of an immorality in the monastic sphere that has been legendary since the Middle Ages. The Bible does state that a person does not have to marry if he does not want to, but no one has the right to enforce that upon those who cannot bear it, for the Scripture also states categorically that it is better to marry than to be in a burning passion.

At the very time this story of the seven priests was told once and never mentioned again, the three part drama, *"CELEBRITY,"* was bring shown on a major network. We did not see the three parts, but we did see the end of the last part and gathered that the entire piece of fictional propaganda was directed against Bible Protestantism. The young man who was the center piece of this drama was a former rapist, who later became a Protestant evangelist. He was shown going kind of berserk. He shot his friend to death for being a homosexual. (Making out Protestant evangelists to be killers instead of portraying the sexual perverts as those who go around killing people, which would be much closer to the truth). At his trial he was stabbed to death by the woman he had formerly raped and left for dead, who apparently had not died. So this whole sorry show was a well orchestrated attempt to denigrate Protestant evangelists.

We recognize that there are unsavory characters in Protestant circles, who make money off the unsuspecting, but are they the only circles where unsavory characters reside? To look at the modern Hollywood movie industry the answer is a resounding yes. It is well then that the actual events of life help to counterbalance the bigoted trash of modern Hollywood and the hypocritical remarks of a Polish Pope.

The enduring nature of Romanism is a sign that it is a devil-inspired conspiracy in a unique sense. After some of the most cruel atrocities of history, combined with the gross immoralities, which have been part and parcel of the whole system, it has still managed not only to survive but to grow.

Cardinal Manning said, "The Catholic Church is either the masterpiece of Satan or the Kingdom of God." Cardinal Newman declared, "Either the Church of Rome is the house of God or the house of Satan."[5] According then to two of its most famous representatives our choices are very limited as to the origin and nature of Romanism. It is either of God or of Satan.

To the Bible-believing Protestant, God is holy and His church is also holy. When the origins of the Roman Catholic church are examined, they point to Satan rather than to Christ. Martin in his book, *"THE RISE AND FALL OF THE ROMAN CHURCH,"* speaks of the method used in electing popes. "Vicious enmities were created. Blood was shed. Lives were taken."[6] He goes on to say:

> At the election of Pope Damasus I in A.D. 366, thirty-seven corpses littered the environs of the Liberian Basilica after a fracas between the followers of Damasus and his archrival, Ursinus.[7]

He goes into much greater detail later on and tells about Pope Stephen bringing his archrival before him with his knee caps broken, his body whipped, and his eyes carved out. He further elaborates:

> Within a year, Pope Stephen will have used Duke Desiderius to get Christophorus, Sergius, and Gratiosus imprisoned, first their eyes cut out, then their lives ended. He then will

turn on Desiderius and by December of 771 will encompass his ruin and death.[8]

Martin again:

> The high point in Marozia's career came at the end of her very long life when she was visited in her Roman prison by an emperor who had just seized possession of the city—Otto III, a successor of Charlemagne. He had only one reason for visiting Marozia—to lay his eyes on the woman who was the mother of a pope, whom she had conceived by another pope, and who was the aunt of a third pope, the grandmother of a fourth pope, and with the help of her own mother, the creator of nine popes in eight years, of whom two had been strangled, one suffocated with a cushion, and four deposed and disposed of in circumstances that have never come to public light.[9]

So reads the pages of Martin's book. Martin still believes in the Roman Catholic Church, but we ask the question how could any one believe that the Roman Cult is the kingdom of God after reading his book and after studying church history? It is absolutely inconceivable that the Holy Spirit of Truth has been connected with such atrocities, crimes, errors, and intrigues, for centuries. It is a spiritual and moral impossibility.

Nevertheless the Vatican has always shown great resiliency and adaptability in keeping abreast of national and international changes. It is working tirelessly toward one goal to bring the entire world to the feet of the Roman Pontiff. The methods used to achieve this goal have included and do include (as we have seen above) murder, massacre, Marxism, propaganda, irenic dialogue, revolution, repression, assassination, education, kindness, coercion, brotherhood, charity, monasticism, enforced celibacy, Jesuit casuistry, intrigue, financial threats and chicanery, and last but certainly not least, a global conspiracy with an historical continuity, and loyal henchmen to see that it continues to endure, unsurpassed in the annals of recorded history. The ends justify the means is no empty slogan, but the modus operandi of the global aspirations of the Jesuits and the Vatican.

As the final stages of the great Satanic religious conspiracy break upon the world, Bible believers need to watch their religious affiliation and fellowship. According to Revelation 18:4, some of God's people are mixed up in the end-time unholy amalgam of Rome's Harlot religion and the one world church. The Word says, ''Come out of her, my people, that you be not partaker of her sins, and receive not of her plagues.'' The one World Church, which will be dominated by Rome and ruled over by the Pope, is looming on the horizon. It may be years before we see the full-orbed picture of Mystery Babylon the Great in its final form, but every true Bible-believer in every generation stands against the Roman Catholic institution, for he sees in it all the seeds of the final apostate conglomerate which is described in Revelation chapters 17-19.

REFERENCES

1. Martin, *RICH CHURCH POOR CHURCH*, p. 13
2. Wilder, John B., *THE SHADOW OF ROME*, Zondervan Pub. Co., Grand Rapids, Mich 1960, p. 87
3. loc. cit.
4. Motley, J. L., *THE RISE OF THE DUTCH REPUBLIC*, Vol I., London, 1913, pp. 294-316
5. Foster, J. M., *THE FUNDAMENTALS, Vol. XI*, p. 113 (in original edition) Chicago, Ill. No date
6. Martin, *THE DECLINE AND FALL OF THE ROMAN CHURCH*, Bantam Books, N.Y. 1981 p. 43
7. loc. cit.
8. Ibid., p. 70
9. Ibid., p. 99

THE WAY OF SALVATION

Salvation is by grace through faith in the finished work of Christ. Dear Reader, if you have never received Christ as your Saviour, you will be lost forever with every other false religionist. Christ died for our sins, and when we turn to Christ, and turn from our sins, and receive His once-for-all sacrifice for our sins by faith, we become a child of God. He died in our place, the just for the unjust, that He might bring us to God. Place all your hope, confidence, faith, and trust in what Christ has done. Turn from your own good works, rituals and practices, and receive by faith alone the finished work of Christ, which alone can satisfy the righteousness of a Holy God, and you will pass from death unto life. Trust the Lord Jesus Christ alone for salvation, see in Him an all sufficient Saviour, one who is able to save unto the uttermost all who come unto God through Him.

It is not the Church which saves nor any sinful man who can do us any good. Only the God-Man, only the Sinless One, the One who fulfilled all righteousness for us, can ever save the sin sick soul. He alone meets God's standards. He alone pays the ransom for our sins in His own body and blood on the cross. He alone is our justification before God. When we receive Christ as Saviour, He becomes our surety before God—He becomes our Righteousness. Trust Him today.

Not the labors of my hands
Can fulfil thy Law's demands
Could my zeal no respite know
Could my tears forever flow
All for sin could not atone
Thou must save, and Thou alone.

Augustus M. Toplady

I am my Beloved's, and My Beloved's mine
He brings a poor vile sinner into His house of Wine
I stand upon his merit, I know no safer stand
Not even where Glory dwelleth, In Immanuel's Land.